My Prayer Journal
Enforcing God's Mandate for My Life

Goshen Publishers LLC
P.O. Box 1562
Stephens City, Virginia 22655
www.GoshenPublishers.com

And the LORD answered me, and said,

Write the vision, and make it plain upon tables,

that he may run that readeth it.

For the vision is yet for an appointed time,

but at the end it shall speak, and not lie:

though it tarry, wait for it;

because it will surely come,

it will not tarry.

Habakkuk 2:2-3

My Prayer Journal
Enforcing God's Mandate for My Life

Apostolic Salutations in the name of our Lord and Savior Jesus Christ.

It is with a strong sense of urgency in my spirit that I sound this clarion call for all of us, as individuals and as a corporate body to seek the Lord through strategic prayer. It is important to record what the Lord is speaking so that you have clarity of direction and formation for your life.

The stakes have never been higher, and the signs are evident that a lot is happening, and the enemy is seriously contending over families, the godly seed, churches, communities, your testimony, and the nations of our world. It is important to take the time to hear from God with an understanding of your divine destiny, purpose, meaning, and assignment.

Use this journal to record what God is speaking regarding your life, the life of your children, the condition of your community, and the state of this world in which we live. I believe that there shall be a performance of everything the Lord has spoken and promised. God will strengthen, comfort, bless and guide you into all truth, wisdom, understanding and fulfillment.

Live long and prosper!

Archbishop Nicholas Duncan-Williams

My Prayer Journal
Enforcing God's Mandate for My Life

100

Affirmations, Declarations, & Quotes

by
Archbishop N. Duncan-Williams

to guide your journey

"Prayer is a necessity for every Christian,
and it is the lifeline of the believer."

"Prayer connects us to God and Him to us."

"Without prayer there is no communication between Heaven and Earth."

"Prayer is what enforces the will of God on the earth and in our lives; so, without prayer, we give the enemy unrestricted access to operate in our lives and communities."

"Prayer gives God legal rights to operate and interfere in our daily lives, because by His own design, God will not operate in the earth realm without man's invitation."

"One thing that we must understand is that prayer is an enforcer. Prayer enforces the promises of God in our lives, but the guarantee of answered prayer is not in the prayer that is prayed, but in the efforts that are put into pleasing God and fulfilling His requirements of us."

"Prayer enforces God's original intent for us and not what we want for ourselves."

"You see, sometimes even though we pray, we don't pray consistently and then we are discouraged when we don't see answers to our prayers, but we must understand that there are opposing forces which must be resisted and held back, so not only is prayer important, but consistent and fervent prayer is key."

"If Jesus withdrew on a regular basis to talk with the Father, this should suggest to us how important prayer is; it was absolutely vital for the Son of God, and it must be absolutely vital for us."

"If you and I don't pray, we give the enemy free access into our lives, our churches, our communities, our health, etc."

"We must pray not only to resist the enemy, but to talk to God, to build ourselves up in faith, and to thank Him for who He is."

"Prayer is the birthplace of the miraculous; the womb of the spirit that transports what eternity has determined to do in time."

"Without prayer God does not have a channel and a means by which He gives expression to what He intends to do among men."

"Jesus said: "Watch and pray..." (Mathew 26:41). The reason many people are not praying is because they are not watching. If you are watching – awake spiritually – you will see the reason to pray."

"Three things open the Heavens: (1) Consistent and persistent prayers; (2) sacrifice; and (3) obedience."

"When we pray, we are standing in the gap for our family, our loved ones, our church, our cities, and the nations of our world."

_____

_____

_____

_____

_____

_____

_____

_____

_____

_____

_____

_____

_____

_____

_____

"Prayer is a supernatural weapon that God has made available to you and me to deploy Him and His angels and to enforce and superimpose His kingdom and His will over the kingdoms of men and over the works of the enemy."

"Pray for strength to always make Jehovah your reference in every decision you make in this life and journey toward your Divine assignment."

"Break the resistance, overturn the workings of the adversary, engage in spiritual warfare, and enforce the victory of the Kingdom of God."

"Prayer is a lifestyle of action that is continual and never stops."

"Prayer is a spiritual discipline and, like every other good discipline, it must be developed and practiced to be effective and meaningful."

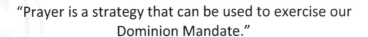

"Prayer is a strategy that can be used to exercise our Dominion Mandate."

"You are commanded to pray always and by daily practice we cultivate a consistent and fervent prayer life."

"The more you pray, you develop stamina and become sensitive to the Voice of God."

"Most people say they desire to know God's will for their life.
I submit to you that His will (His expression of the future)
is for you to pray."

_____

_____

_____

_____

_____

_____

_____

_____

_____

_____

_____

_____

_____

_____

_____

_____

_____

_____

_____

_____

"We have to pray for the salvation of others and for them to receive the Spirit of adoption. We obtained grace because someone prayed for us."

"Commit to the spiritual discipline of prayer and remain aware of the adversary and the plans that have been set up for your demise."

"Deploy the blood of Jesus, the release of ministering angels to secure the recovery of your stolen goods, treasuries, fortunes, wealth and blessings."

"Terminate, abolish, and cancel strange happenings accidents, incidents, evil storms, impending dangers, and contrary winds in Jesus' name."

"Override ill-wills, evil imaginations and expectations, satanic pregnancies against the righteous, God's people and His church, our community, and the nations of our world."

"Command the will, purpose and the counsel of God for our lives, families, finances, communities, churches, and nations to prevail and be superimposed over and against every agenda of the enemy."

"There is no substitute for prayer."

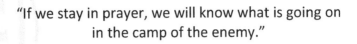

"If we stay in prayer, we will know what is going on in the camp of the enemy."

"If we spend time with God, we will spend less time with the enemy."

"When you develop a prayer life, God will give you divine secrets."

"Prayer is a daily necessity for daily triumph."

"If you pray, you can withstand anything."

"Without prayer God does not have a channel or a means by which to give expression to what He intends to do among men."

"We shouldn't only pray in bad times; we should pray in good times so that bad times never come."

"Jesus said: "Watch and pray..." (Matthew 26:41). The reason many folks are not praying is because they are not watching. If you are watching – awake spiritually – you will see the reason to pray."

"As much as teaching and preaching are great, teaching and preaching do not bring revival. They educate, illuminate, enlighten, and empower; but it is prayer that brings revival."

"Prayer is a supernatural weapon that God has made available to you and me to deploy Him and His angels and to enforce and superimpose His kingdom and His will over the kingdoms of men and over the works of the enemy."

_____
_____
_____
_____
_____
_____
_____
_____
_____
_____
_____
_____
_____
_____
_____
_____

"Prayer is a discipline and like every other good discipline,
it must be developed."

"Prayer is a strategy that can be used to exercise our Dominion Mandate."

_____

_____

_____

_____

_____

_____

_____

_____

_____

_____

_____

_____

_____

_____

_____

_____

_____

"You are commanded to pray always and by daily practice you cultivate a consistent and fervent prayer life."

_____

_____

_____

_____

_____

_____

_____

_____

_____

_____

_____

_____

_____

_____

_____

_____

_____

"The more you pray; you develop stamina and become sensitive to the Voice of God."

"Most people say they desire to know God's will for their life.
I submit to you that His will (His expression of the future) is
for you to pray."

_____

_____

_____

_____

_____

_____

_____

_____

_____

_____

_____

_____

_____

_____

_____

_____

"We have to pray for others to be saved and receive the Spirit of adoption. We got in because someone prayed for us."

"Beloved, our Savior had to fast and pray to deal with Satan. How much more must those of us who are born-again believers do?"

"We discipline the flesh through times of fasting and prayer."

"Prayer is the most important privilege of a Christian and should be the heart desire of a new life in Christ."

_____

_____

_____

_____

_____

_____

_____

_____

_____

_____

_____

_____

_____

_____

_____

_____

"More is accomplished by prayer than has ever been accomplished
by all the other "religious activities" in the world."

"It is by prayer that we enforce the "joy of His salvation."

"Prayer is dependence on God – not on self."

"To pray is as much a part of the Christian life as breathing is to the natural life."

"If we would spend time in prayer,
we would always have revelation."

"Prayer is a daily necessity for daily triumph."

"When I took control of my pain and submitted it to the Lord in prayer, the mercies of God were extended to me."

"Without praying your pain into God's hands there can be no turning of your pain into effective use."

"Brethren, I can only encourage you not to dwell on any pain, not to nurse it or feed it with self-pity, but to cast your pain unto the Lord by prayer."

_____

_____

_____

_____

_____

_____

_____

_____

_____

_____

_____

_____

_____

_____

_____

_____

_____

"Turn your pain into a live conduit of prayer and let your soul be restored and empowered."

"Seeking the Lord by waiting on Him through fasting and prayer is a wonderful and powerful tool
in understanding God's timing for one's life."

"Through prayers and fasting you can also understand divine timing for your life and live a victorious Christian life."

"Any time you are determined to seek God's face and pray with fasting, you will hear His voice, which will give you direction and insight into the times and seasons."

"By prayer, claim the whole armor of God as your spiritual clothing."

"As you pray in the spirit, The Holy Spirit helps you to pray about issues beyond your human understanding."

"Prayer is a powerful weapon when we pray with petitions and supplications."

"Prayer is communication with God.
Communication is a two-way flow of information."

"*Prayer* is talking to God and God talking back to you."

"No other spiritual weapon substitutes the place of fervent prayer."

"Jesus Christ, our High Priest, commands us to pray and not faint."

"Employ the weapon of endless, ceaseless prayers with the Word of God and all satanic obstacles will give way for a full manifestation and demonstration of God's purpose for your life."

_____

_____

_____

_____

_____

_____

_____

_____

_____

_____

_____

_____

_____

_____

_____

"A wise and Godly mother covers her child in prayer because she knows that there are no limits to the power of prayer."

"Prayer changes things and people."

"The Bible commands us to pray without ceasing."

"God is calling us to pray and stand our ground, to take battle to the enemy's camp, and to retrieve everything that the enemy has stolen from us."

"Prayer is the cord that keeps us connected to the Father, our Source."

"The time has come for men to rise up go back to the basics
and learn to pray."

"Watch the life of a man who prays.
Regardless of how low he may fall, he always bounces back."

"Inner strength is the result of time spent with God in prayer."

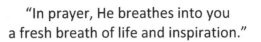

"In prayer, He breathes into you
a fresh breath of life and inspiration."

"Prayer generates total dependence on God."

"Prayer is a power producer and strength builder."

"Pray when we think we know the solution to a problem, and pray when we cannot find any answers."

"There is no convenient time to pray. We simply pray – always."

"Praying daily means walking in His mercies daily."

"There is an important ingredient in prayer that is imperative if we are to receive answers to our prayers.
This ingredient is an obstinate adamancy to stay in consistent and prevalent prayer without wavering."

"Prayer is hard work. Prayer is sweat and blood."

"Prayer drains you naturally but renews you spiritually."

"It is not easy to cultivate a lifestyle of prayer.
But it is worth the effort."

"Prayer has kept the weakened knots tied together
in the areas that threatened to break."

"Impatience will not work well if you are going to take up your God-given responsibility of praying ceaselessly."

"The Church prayed for Peter and an Angel was released."

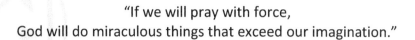

"If we will pray with force,
God will do miraculous things that exceed our imagination."

"It is through prayer that the prison doors are opened."

"It is only by prayer that we open the Gates to nations."

"We must pray in this generation to release and strengthen the five-fold ministry giftings."

"When you as a believer pronounce through a declaration in prayer, you are enforcing the blessing, which the Spirit has already revealed (1 John 1:3-5)."

"When we accept the assignment to pray and stand in the gap for individuals, for churches, for nations, etc., we move from just merely watching in prayer – we are elevated to the position of Intercessor."

"Prayer breaks all limits!"

Made in USA - North Chelmsford, MA
1073003_9781948233026
04.07.2020 1101